W9-BGV-522

Heroes, Legends . . . Dads

Other Books by Joe Garner

We Interrupt This Broadcast
And the Crowd Goes Wild
And the Fans Roared
Echoes of Notre Dame Football
Stay Tuned
Now Showing
Made You Laugh
Life Is Like a Box of Chocolates

Heroes, Legends...Dads

Eight Inspiring Stories of Superstar Athletes and Their Dads

JOE GARNER

Andrews McMeel Publishing

Kansas City

05 06 07 08 09 INL 10 9 8 7 6 5 4 3 2 1

Library of Congress Cataloging-in-Publication Data

Garner, Joe.
    Heroes, legends—dads : eight inspiring stories of superstar athletes and their dads / Joe Garner.
        p. cm.
    ISBN 0-7407-4178-0
    1. Athletes—United States—Family relationships. 2. Athletes—United States—Biography. 3. Father and child—United States. I. Title.

GV697.A1G37 2005
796'.092'273—dc22
[B]
                                                                                            2005041101

Attention: Schools and Businesses

Andrews McMeel books are available at quantity discounts with bulk purchase for educational, business, or sales promotional use. For information, please write to: Special Sales Department, Andrews McMeel Publishing, 4520 Main Street, Kansas City, Missouri 64111.

To Dad,

for all that you are . . .

for all that you do

CONTENTS

ACKNOWLEDGMENTS

Just like in sports—putting a book together takes a team effort. I'm lucky to be playing with one of the best—Andrews McMeel Publishing—including Chris Schillig and her wonderfully creative staff and designers Tim Lynch and Holly Camerlinck, copy chief Michelle Daniel, and administrative assistant JuJu Johnson, Kristine Campbell, and Courtney Moilanen, and the rest of the tenacious cheerleading squad in the AMP publicity department.

A special thank you to Abigail Ray, the greatest utility player I could ever ask for. Thanks to my agent, Sloan Harris.

I am grateful to Chris Monte for his masterful editing, and Jim Castle and Robert Dixon for their ingenuity in the menu and graphic design for the DVD.

I am also grateful to my bookkeeper Janel Syverud for her support and encouragement.

I am particularly grateful to Louise Argianas at ABC Sports, Max Segal at HBO, Linda Sponaugle at NFL Films, Joy Dellapina at NBA Entertainment, Jennifer Greechan at Major League Baseball Productions, and Greg Ramsey at NASCAR Images for permitting me to include these memorable sports moments.

Thank you to the following people for providing the very best photographs: Chad Witt at Getty Images, Jenni Rosenthal at AP Wide World, Cora Bauer at Landov LLC, Eddie Roche at Motorsports Images & Archives, and Jodi Helman at *Sports Illustrated:* www.sipictures.com.

And finally, my heartfelt thanks for my home team, Colleen, James (J. B.), and Jillian. Thank you to my parents Jim (a wonderful dad) and Betty Garner, and to Jerry and Sandi Barnes for their love and support.

INTRODUCTION

Professional athletes have always held a special place in our imagination. From the time we were kids, we have reveled in their exploits, venerated them like royalty, and fantasized about being them. They have become our modern-day heroes, their triumphs and tribulations the stuff of legend.

Yet as extraordinary as these athletic superstars may be, many would never have reached the pinnacle of their sport—or become such an inspiration to the rest of us— had it not been for the influence of one remarkable individual: their dad. He was often the first to spot their talent, the first to teach them to pitch, to swing a bat, or throw a punch. He was there to cheer them on to victory and to console them in defeat. And to this day, despite their tremendous fame and fortune, what still matters most to these athletes is their father's approval.

Heroes, Legends . . . Dads offers an intimate and admiring look at how the lives and careers of eight exceptional athletes have been shaped by their fathers. Packed with intriguing interviews, thrilling sports highlights, and moving personal anecdotes, the book and accompanying DVD get to the heart of these inspiring, sometimes contentious, but always compelling relationships.

These portraits strip away the stardom and the hoopla, revealing the very human bond between some of the world's best-known sports personalities and their dads. You'll experience the joys and frustrations of second-generation stars like slugger Barry Bonds, All-Pro quarterback Peyton Manning, and basketball phenom Luke Walton as they emerge from the shadows of their legendary fathers; the fiery relationship between boxing champ Oscar De La Hoya and his father, Joel, who urged

Oscar into the ring as a spindly six-year-old; the intense and not always welcome dedication of Doug Finch to the softball career of his daughter, Jennie; and the entertaining tale of NASCAR legend Dale Jarrett, who slogged through an assortment of odd jobs, including a stint as a goat herder, before heeding his stock-car-racing father's advice to join the family business.

What you'll discover in each instance is the seminal role these athletes' fathers played in nurturing their talents and, more importantly, molding their character. At their core, these stories may very well mirror your own father-child relationship, with all the same frictions, loyalty, love, and support.

In the years since the release of my two previous multimedia sports compilations, I have heard from hundreds of people about the deep connection sports have provided in their relationships with their fathers. *Heroes, Legends . . . Dads* is a testament to that bond, and these inspiring stories and riveting, emotional DVD moments will undoubtedly continue to enrich your relationship for years to come.

Heroes, Legends . . . Dads

"I kind of went the other way. I never coached my sons. I never pushed. Sometimes I think, if you do that, you just screw them up."

ONE

Archie and Peyton Manning

FIERCE COMPETITORS, LOVING FAMILY

It's not easy raising a superstar—even if you were once a pretty big star yourself.

Archie Manning, who played quarterback and was a two-time All-American at the University of Mississippi and then went on to play for fourteen seasons in the NFL, could see that his middle son, Peyton, had both the talent and the passion to be a successful athlete himself. But Archie knew that passion had to be properly channeled if Peyton was to ultimately succeed.

So Archie, who preferred to remain a spectator while his three sons pursued their athletic careers, stepped in when Peyton got in the face of his basketball coach.

The team had lost their first game and the coach told the players it was because they weren't mentally ready.

"The reason we lost," Peyton shot back, "is that you don't know what you are doing."

Peyton was eleven at the time.

Archie, in his usual spot in the background as the

team met, saw his son speak up, but couldn't hear what Peyton was saying. So, on the drive home, Archie asked Peyton what he had told his coach.

Scr-e-e-e-ch.

When Peyton repeated what he said, Archie hit the brakes, made a U-turn, and took Peyton to the home of George Fowler, the volunteer coach. There, at Archie's firm insistence, a chagrined Peyton apologized.

Archie never liked getting involved.

"I know there are a lot of fathers out there who coach their sons and want them to be in athletics," Archie said. "I kind of went the other way. I never coached my sons. I never pushed. Sometimes I think, if you do that, you just screw them up."

Archie didn't have to push his sons—Cooper, Peyton, and Eli—into cleats. His own career did that through osmosis.

Who wouldn't want to follow in their father's footsteps if those footsteps had left a lasting impression on football fields all over this country?

The Mannings still have an old, worn videotape of Peyton telling a television reporter in New Orleans, where his father was playing for the Saints at the time, that he wanted to be a quarterback.

Peyton was three.

In those years, it was common to see Peyton and Cooper, who was two years older, running around the Saints' practice field pretending they were in a game, rolled-up wads of discarded tape serving as a makeshift football.

Cooper's dreams of football success ended early. A congenital back problem forced him to give up the game in his freshman year at his father's alma mater. The future in professional football for Eli, five years younger than Peyton, has just begun after a record-breaking career at Mississippi. Drafted No. 1 by the San Diego Chargers, he refused to play for them, forcing the Chargers to trade Eli to the New York Giants where he experienced the normal frustrations of a rookie.

It is Peyton, playing for the Indianapolis Colts, who has not only emulated his father, but already surpassed him.

It was assumed Peyton would go to Mississippi. How could a Manning go anywhere else? But at the time Manning's high school career was coming to an end, the Mississippi football program was facing probation and, as if that wasn't bad enough, the team simply wasn't very good.

AUGUST 26, 1996
$3.50 (CAN. $3.95)

Sports Illustrated

College Football '96

**IN HIS FATHER'S IMAGE:
PEYTON MANNING
IDOL OF No. 1 TENNESSEE**

Sports Illustrated

SEPTEMBER 14, 1970   60 CENTS

TOP 20 IN COLLEGE FOOTBALL

**Archie Manning
Idol of Ole Miss**

So Peyton studied the media guides of prospective colleges and vigorously questioned the coaches who recruited him about everything from the qualifications of their assistants to the number of returning letterman they would have. Ultimately, Peyton chose the University of Tennessee.

And despite his natural desire to see his son put on the same uniform he had worn with such distinction,

Archie supported Peyton. He had spent too many years on too many bad teams to encourage his son to join yet another one.

After a brilliant career at Tennessee, where he set two NCAA, eight Southeastern Conference, and thirty-three school records, Peyton was picked No. 1 in the 1998 NFL draft by the Indianapolis Colts.

With his mastery of the offense, his quick release,

and his laserlike passing accuracy, Peyton has also been a record-setting quarterback in the NFL—not only the best in the game today, but, arguably, among the best who have ever played the game. With those horseshoes on his helmet and the touchdown passes sailing from his arm, he has stirred memories of the legendary figure who once wore another helmet with the horseshoes on it, Johnny Unitas of the Baltimore Colts.

Archie never achieved those heights, and despite his considerable skills, he was never fortunate enough in his years with the Saints, the Houston Oilers, and the Minnesota Vikings to play on a championship-caliber team.

Yet, no matter how many fans fawn over Peyton, no matter how many media members praise him, one opinion matters more than all the others: his father's.

If Archie is not at a game—he tries to give equal time to Peyton and Eli—Peyton will find a way to escape the crush of humanity that surrounds him after a game, plant himself in a quiet spot, pull out his cell phone, and call Archie to get his father's view of his performance.

Archie is just as close with Eli and with Cooper, now a New Orleans businessman.

Archie's father committed suicide when Archie was in college, and Peyton has spoken of that dark memory that has pushed Archie to stay close to his own sons.

"Dad and I haven't talked much about him losing his father," Peyton said. "He was a lot older than my dad, and they never had this super close relationship."

But that closeness still ends where the playing field begins, just as it always had when his sons were young. Asked before Eli's first start with the Giants if he had any advice for his youngest son, Archie told the *New York Daily News,* "I don't get into that. That's why he's got coaches. He's a big boy. He doesn't need me. I don't do that. I don't play quarterback daddy. I'm his daddy."

Eli understands his father's approach and appreciates it.

"You see a lot of parents who are trying to live their football dream through their son . . . where my father [already] experienced his," Eli has said. "He went all the way and did his thing and he wanted us to experience ours and not get involved."

Still, Archie admits, he really can't stay detached. "I know when I played, I had a nervous stomach," Archie said. "When my children play, I get the same deal."

Archie's stomach was really nervous on December 26, 2004, and it wasn't caused by watching Peyton. Rather it was the thought that he wouldn't see his son play at all.

Peyton was involved in the most memorable game of his career, bidding to break Dan Marino's record of forty-eight touchdown passes in a single season. When Peyton began that game at the RCA Dome in Indianapolis against the San Diego Chargers with forty-seven touchdown passes, Archie and his wife, Olivia, were stuck in an airport in Memphis.

They had planned to make the trip from their New Orleans home to Indianapolis the night before, but bad weather had grounded them. They tried again Sunday

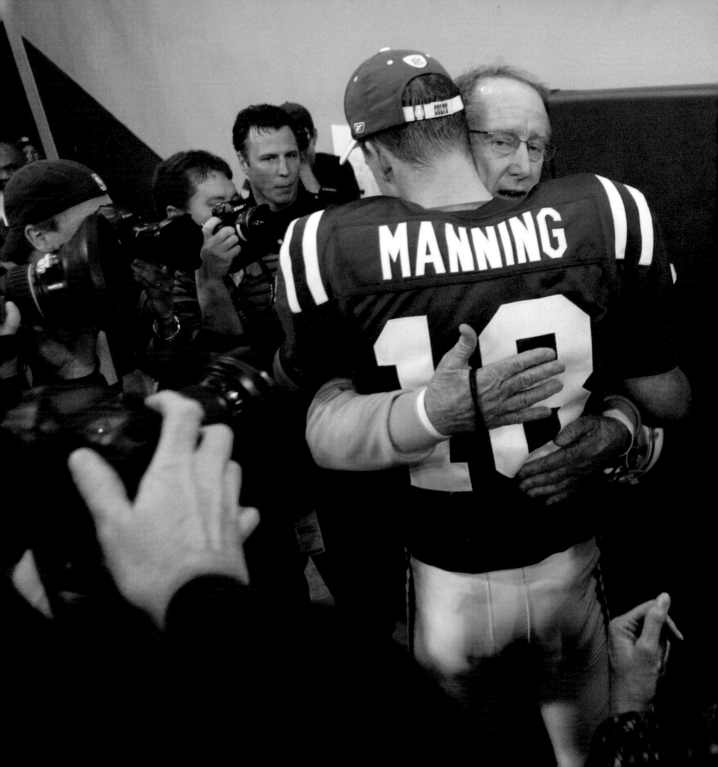

morning but, because of a tardy flight attendant, missed their connecting flight in Memphis. Jim Irsay, owner of the Colts, dispatched his private jet to pick up the Mannings.

They weren't there when Peyton threw his record-tying forty-eighth TD pass in the third quarter. But they did arrive with nine minutes remaining in the game.

And when Peyton connected with Brandon Stokley on the record-breaking forty-ninth TD pass, a twenty-one-yarder with fifty-six seconds to play, there was Archie in a tunnel by the end zone, squinting because he was too nervous to fully watch until it was clear the play was going to be successful.

"Mannings don't get mushy," Archie said afterward, "but we are just so proud of him."

Their closeness is mirrored again and again. When Eli was drafted first by the Chargers, the Mannings became the only family in pro football history to have three of its members become first-round picks. Archie was selected No. 2 by the Saints in 1971.

And the trio also has another football bond—this one downright eerie. Eli's first touchdown was a six-yarder. Archie's first touchdown pass also went for six yards. Peyton's first touchdown throw? Yep, six yards.

There's an old cliché about the apple not falling far from the tree. But on the Manning family tree, they even fall the same distance.

"I had no choice. It was do or die.
Obviously I didn't want to disappoint
myself by losing a fight, but to
disappoint my father, oh my gosh,
that was the worst thing I could
ever do to him."

TWO

Joel and Oscar De La Hoya

A FATHER'S TOUGH LOVE BUILDS A CHAMPION

De La Hoya had dreams of becoming a boxer, of following in his father's footsteps, of even someday surpassing his father by becoming a champion.

Those were the dreams of *Joel* De La Hoya, whose father, Vincente, had also been a boxer.

The dreams of Joel's youngest son, Oscar, were different. Oscar wanted to sing like his mother, Cecilia. He wanted to paint. He wanted to develop his creative side.

But all that came to end on a life-altering afternoon when Oscar was seven.

"I had followed my brother to a baseball park," said Oscar, who grew up in East Los Angeles. "It was a Saturday. My brother was always pursuing his goal of becoming a major leaguer."

Oscar, who was two years younger than his brother, Joel Jr., was happy to tag along. Happy until he was jarringly

interrupted when his father pulled up in the family car. Joel Sr. got out, got Oscar, and put him in the front seat.

"You know what," Joel told his young son, "you're not playing baseball. You're gonna be a fighter. You're gonna be a boxer."

It wasn't quite as simple as that. Forget the image of the adult Oscar, stalking his opponents in the ring with the look of a killer, his smooth hands and dancing feet moving in concert with the rhythm of a Fred Astaire, Oscar's jaw effectively weathering blows that would knock a lesser man senseless.

From the time boxing gloves had first been put on Oscar at the age of three, his first inclination when he was hit was to cry. His second inclination was to run.

But that all began to change after that day in the park.

Oscar didn't try to blur his father's vision, didn't sneak back to the baseball field, and didn't stray from the path his father had put him on.

"From that day on," Oscar said, "I decided this is what I wanted to do. This is the sport I decided I was going to excel at and really become somebody."

Joel had originally pushed Joel Jr. into the ring, but eventually baseball won out. So, he turned to Oscar.

"When I saw my father dedicate his whole life into making sure his son becomes a great champion in the future, I said to myself, 'Hey, why not make my father happy?' I figured I could always be a singer later."

Still, there was no guarantee Joel's dream of a championship for Oscar would ever become more than that.

There had been no titles for Vincente, a featherweight in the 1940s, who fought mostly in his native Mexico. Joel's own championship aspirations were interrupted by the more compelling aspiration of putting food on the table for his young family. A lightweight, Joel won nine of his thirteen professional fights with one draw, but he hung up the gloves when he found it impossible to juggle a job and the demands of a heavy training schedule.

And so, like many other fathers in many other gyms around East Los Angeles, Joel poured his dashed hopes into his son.

For the De La Hoyas, the Eastside Boxing Club was their launching pad.

"I was programmed to succeed," Oscar said. "I had no choice. It was do or die. Obviously I didn't want to disappoint myself by losing a fight, but to disappoint my

father, oh my gosh, that was the worst thing I could ever do to him."

By the age of nine, Oscar was a neighborhood sensation. After he won a local tournament, family, friends, and neighbors smothered him with congratulations and wild predictions about his future. Oscar soaked in every word, every pat on the back.

"I would practice my signature," he said, "so that I could give out autographs someday. I would have family members interview me so I could be prepared for what was ahead."

But he was still waiting for the praise he most desperately wanted—the praise from his father. Oscar, however, was in for a long wait. Joel felt that if he were to fill his son's ego, it would deflate his will to seek even higher levels. So he withheld his praise. And Oscar fought harder to get it. It was a pattern that would continue well into Oscar's professional career.

Oscar's focus at the end of his amateur career, however, was on his mother, not his father. She was his biggest cheerleader, rooting him on as he battled his way along the road to the 1992 Olympics.

It was a road whose end Cecilia never saw. Nearly two years before the Barcelona Olympics, Cecilia died of breast cancer. She was just thirty-nine.

On Cecilia's deathbed, Oscar promised his mother he would win an Olympic gold medal. Initially, however, he did not pour his grief and anger into the punching bag.

"I actually quit for several months after she passed

away," Oscar said. "I told myself, 'My mother's not here. Why am I going to do this? Why am I going to go out there and risk my life up in the ring? There's no reason for it.'

"But one day, I just realized that, hey, if she were here, she would want her son to go out there and win the gold. So my father and I became even closer. We trained harder together. We pushed ourselves to our limits. We made sure that we were going to come back home with that gold medal."

The glory days when gold seemed to glitter everywhere on the U.S. boxing team were long gone by 1992.

"I was watching my Olympic teammates losing, one right after another," Oscar said.

But Oscar didn't lose, reaching the gold-medal round where he faced Marco Rudolph. Oscar knew Rudolph all too well. He had been beaten by the German the year before at the world championships in Australia, Oscar's only loss over a five-year period.

"It was the scariest moment that I had ever felt in my life," Oscar said, "to think of not fulfilling my mother's dream. If I didn't win the gold medal, I would have quit boxing."

But win he did, by a 7–2 score, and his father, who was in the stands, cried.

Oscar returned home a hero, the only American fighter that year with Olympic gold around his neck. More gold, in terms of wealth, beckoned for boxing's new Golden Boy—and, it seemed, the championships his father had long coveted.

Who would train Oscar? Who would manage him? Who would promote him? The line stretched around the corner. Everybody wanted a piece of him.

And what about his father, the man who had put him on this golden path?

"Things changed," Oscar said, "once the big money was involved. People were manipulating my father, trying to get him to get me to sign a contract. They would tell him, 'If he doesn't sign, his career is over and he's not going to have anything. He's going to be left in the streets with zero.'

"My father was scared that we would be left with nothing. I said I wasn't going to sign. It got kind of nasty between my father and me for a few months.

"But then one day, we realized no amount of money is going to pull us apart. Those were the most difficult moments of our relationship. It was tough. But we came out of it stronger. Our love, our unity overcame all."

Oscar eventually wound up with promoter Bob Arum, who brilliantly marketed him, protecting him early in his career with easy opponents, then matching him against bigger names who had passed their prime before finally matching Oscar with the best fighters of his era. Arum made Oscar the richest nonheavyweight ever by taking advantage of his crossover appeal on two levels. Blessed with movie-star good looks, Oscar not only drew more women than any other contemporary fighter, but also appealed to the growing Hispanic market.

Those championships belts Joel had dreamed of

began to fill up Oscar's trophy case, from 130 pounds—eventually up to 160.

Praise flowed from all corners—all but one.

His father, the man he had been trying to please all his life, still wouldn't acknowledge his son's greatness. A frustrated Oscar said he would exchange all his belts for a few simple words of praise from his father.

"When I was winning fights and winning world titles," Oscar said, "my father was always the one to criticize me. He would tell me, 'You know that was fine, but we are going to do better the next time.' I was always looking for the words, 'Son, you did well. Son, I'm very happy for you. Son, I'm very proud of you.'"

Oscar didn't hear those words for his first thirty-one professional fights, all victories. He finally heard them on the night of September 18, 1999, in a dressing room at Las Vegas' Mandalay Bay Events Center—after suffering his first loss on a majority decision to Felix Trinidad.

"My father saw the pain in my face," Oscar said. "He knew what I had been through. And he told me, 'I am very proud of you, of what you had accomplished in the ring.' I found that he did have feelings. He felt I had accomplished all the goals, all the dreams—all the hard work and sweat had paid off. It was a very special moment.

"My father used the macho way, the tough way, because that's how he grew up. But with my kids, I tell them they are the best right from the get-go. I give them that hug they need every single day."

"Go out and have fun. We'll be proud
of you no matter what. If you want to
be a baseball player, that's fine."

THREE

Ken Griffey and Ken Griffey Jr.

FRIENDS ON THE FIELD, TEAMMATES FOR LIFE

A dad can always tell. He can look into his son's eyes and see that steely determination, that stubborn setting of the ways. And so, on Friday, September 14, 1990, as George Kenneth Griffey Senior approached George Kenneth Griffey Junior, he saw something that convinced him that a home run was coming, a historic home run. Senior, who had only recently joined his son with the Seattle Mariners, had just blasted a long ball and now Junior was about to make them baseball's only father-son duo ever to homer in the same game—much less to hit back-to-back homers.

"I felt for him then," Senior said after the game. "I knew he would be thinking home run. I could see it in his eyes when I crossed the plate. He tried to do it after I hit the other two against Oakland and in Boston. I knew he would be trying awfully hard. So I just sat quietly and hoped he relaxed and got a pitch he could hit. Then boom."

"It's something I didn't think we'd ever do," Junior

said at the time. "In the dugout, I slapped some hands and traded some high-fives, then I hugged him. Actually, he hugged me."

It was a magical moment for baseball fans, but it was especially powerful for the Griffeys, because Ken Sr. had always strived to build a strong relationship with his son even though his career took him on the road for weeks

at a time. The driving force behind their bond was not a shared love of baseball but Ken Sr.'s frustration over his lack of a connection to his own father.

Robert "Buddy" Griffey was a fine high school athlete and ballplayer. But he failed as a parent, leaving his wife and six children behind in Donora, Pennsylvania, to scrape by on welfare. After the age of two, Ken Sr. would see his father only two more times in his life—once at the age of nine and then at seventeen. Ken received his baseball guidance as a youth from Buddy's former Donora High School teammate, Stan Musial.

During high school, Ken was hoping for a football scholarship to college but when his girlfriend Alberta (Birdie) told him she was pregnant, he did what he felt was the honorable thing and married her. So, when the Cincinnati Reds drafted him, Ken was more than glad to sign. He struggled in the minor leagues but was encouraged by his mother and brothers. During the winters he worked minimum-wage jobs in a print shop and a steel mill and supplemented his meager income with welfare. He was determined to give his baby, Ken Jr. (and later another son, Craig), more than he had ever had. That determination and hard work led to his major league career and enabled Junior to grow up with the breezy confidence that helped make him a superstar.

"He's not only a great player, he's a great guy," Junior has said about his dad. Ken was determined to do better by his boys even in the simple act of calling from road trips to tell them he loved them. "If they needed me or

something happened to them, I would be there," he once said. "They know that."

Regardless of his monumental talent, the young carefree star—who reached the majors at only nineteen—lacked the intensity, work ethic, and dedication to fundamentals of his father, the result of a childhood with plenty of love, instead of hard knocks. Senior never cared what others said, he saw a happy son gradually maturing. "Spoiled or whatever, I did what I had to do and I was behind them all the way. I didn't have that with my father."

Senior never pushed Junior into sports. "He was a dad," Junior has said. "That was it." But he did encourage

him, letting him hang around the ballpark and the great players on Cincinnati's Big Red Machine—Johnny Bench, Pete Rose, Tony Perez, Joe Morgan.

"Dad never forced the issue with any of us," Junior said at the start of his career. "If I wanted to come to a game, I did. If I didn't, I didn't have to. He said, 'Go out and have fun. We'll be proud of you no matter what. If you want to be a baseball player, that's fine.' It's just something I've always wanted to do and have been fortunate enough to be good at."

And when Junior wanted to learn baseball, Senior encouraged him but also taught him to understand the game—its drills, its routines, its mechanics—like a professional even from the age of eight. He was certainly learning from a pro. Senior played on two World Series championship teams in Cincinnati. In 1976 he hit .336 and finished second in the league. He played in three All-Star Games. He won the Most Valuable Player Award in the 1980 event. On his way to more than 2,000 hits and 2,000 games over nineteen seasons, Senior eventually played with the New York Yankees, the Atlanta Braves, and Cincinnati again. He became respected and beloved in clubhouses as a wise presence who freely gave advice to young players.

Junior was a star from the start—at age ten he reached base in every at bat in the first eleven games of his Little League season. He only struggled, it seemed, when he tried too hard to impress his dad. "From twelve to seventeen, he very seldom saw me play because he was

[in the major leagues]," Junior said years later. "So, every time he'd come to town, I'm trying to hit the ball 700 feet. I'd strike out and he would laugh."

The rest of the time Ken Jr. impressed just about everyone else, soaring through the Mariners' farm system making his major league debut at age nineteen, and becoming an All-Star at age twenty. In the 1990 season, Griffey was brimming with charisma and potential. However, no one was positive that he would go on to hit more than 500 homers, including two seasons with fifty-six roundtrippers, or that during the 1990s he'd routinely compete with Barry Bonds for the title of baseball's best player.

Meanwhile, as the Reds raced toward a World Series title in 1990, Senior was buried on the bench, batting just .206. Finally, he asked for and eventually got his release, enabling Seattle to sign him on August 29, making the Griffeys teammates.

"This is the pinnacle for me, something I'm very proud of," Senior said. "You can talk about the '76 batting race, the two World Series I played in, and the All-Star Games I played in, but this is No. 1. This is the best thing that's ever happened to me."

Even before his first spring training in 1989, Junior was kidding around telling his dad they'd be teammates one day. When the opportunity arose, he helped make it happen. "I didn't ask for him," Junior said in 1990, acknowledging that he'd pushed management to trade for his dad all year long. "It was more of a demand on my part. I just told Senior to get over here. I wanted him around."

Senior confessed that he'd long thought about playing alongside his son but that he wasn't sure it would ever happen and certainly not so quickly. "This all happened because of what Junior has done," he said. "I

never thought he'd make it to the big leagues as quickly as he did, and I'm proud of him."

So the first father and son duo to play in the majors simultaneously were now teammates. Nobody felt the pressure more than the father. "That first night was the most nerve-racking night I've ever spent in my life," Senior said. "It took a lot more concentration and emotional restraint than I could have ever imagined. When I first went to the bat rack, I had to lean on it to steady myself. . . . Then I go to the plate and I heard, 'Come on, Dad!' That really shook me up."

But Senior came through, lining a base hit, and Junior followed with a single of his own. Afterward, Senior called the experience "the most weird and wonderful feeling a man can have" but added that it was a thrill not just to make history but because the two men were so close.

"I understand that a lot of kids simply can't stand being around their fathers, but that's not the case with me and Junior," he said. "I enjoy being around him, and he enjoys being around me." Observing that their relationship evolved into one more like brothers, Ken Sr. said, "He's asked me for a lot more advice than he ever asked before. We talk a lot more than we did before."

It would only get better after that first game.

Senior—who lived in Junior's house that last month—played inspired baseball, hitting .377 the rest of the season, and his presence also seemed to lift the entire team. The Mariners won five of their first six games after he arrived and ultimately raised their team average to .275 in September from .233 in August. The following season Senior would stick around as a part-time player and help guide Junior in his breakthrough season. He would subsequently be hired as the Mariners' hitting coach and later—when Junior got himself traded home to Cincinnati so he could be near his own children—Ken Sr. would become the Reds' hitting coach.

Nothing, of course, could top the night of September 14. In the first inning, after Angels pitcher Kirk McCaskill walked leadoff hitter Harold Reynolds, Senior ripped an 0–2 changeup 402 feet to center field. It would be the second-to-last home run of his career. McCaskill then fell behind Junior 3–0. Normally a hitter would take a pitch in that situation, but manager Jim Lefebreve, sensing the potential for history, flashed the hit sign. And Griffey hit it—388 feet to the opposite field. The Angels came back to win the game but their triumph was overshadowed by the emotional thrill of the Griffeys' accomplishment.

"It's everything that everyone has probably dreamed about at one time or another, and now we're living it," Senior said later, adding that he was moved by how this powerful experience seemed to have a universal resonance. "Everyone who comes up to me now tells me they have a different relationship with their sons after they've seen us together."

"Find the passion for something
and do that. You don't need to play
basketball because I did."

FOUR

Bill and Luke Walton

RADICAL FATHER, CONSERVATIVE SON

The name Walton invokes sharp and varied images to a basketball fan. There is the red-haired hippie protesting the Vietnam War or relishing a Grateful Dead concert. There is the unstoppable UCLA Bruin, making an incredible twenty-one of twenty-two shots and scoring forty-four points en route to leading his team to the NCAA championship in 1973—one of two won by UCLA in the Walton era. Then there is the Walton of the Portland Trail Blazers, awash in a sea of red as he celebrates the only championship ever won by that franchise.

But to the contemporary fan, those are faded images from three decades ago, the images of Bill Walton. Today, the name Walton invokes the image of son Luke, a clean-cut youngster, perfecting his craft in Laker purple and gold, fortunate enough to have had Shaquille O'Neal, Kobe Bryant, Karl Malone, and Gary Payton as teammates in his rookie season. Yes, there was turmoil on that 2003–04 team, but there was also a chance for a first-year player to learn from superstars. And from a superstar coach, Phil Jackson, winner of a record-tying nine NBA titles.

But of course, when it comes to learning from the great ones, Luke started soaking in hoop knowledge at a very early age from his dad.

Luke seemed destined to play the game from the day he came into this world, when he was named Luke, after Maurice Lucas, the menacing power forward Luke's father played with on the Trail Blazers.

Along with the name, Luke's father passed along his genes. Although Luke wouldn't quite grow to his father's six foot eleven, he would reach six foot eight, big enough to leave his own mark on the court.

Luke would eventually try to follow in his father's footsteps, but at first he didn't realize just how big those footsteps were.

"Growing up, he was always a star," Luke said, "but we thought that was normal. People would ask for his autograph, but it wasn't until elementary school, junior high that I first realized he was one of the great basketball players."

Until then, Bill, by then a member of the Boston Celtics with his best days behind him because of chronic foot problems, was just a lesser light in Luke's eyes.

"My favorite player growing up was Larry Bird," Luke said. "I used to love watching Magic, watching the Lakers and Celtics play against each other. My dad was just some guy on the team we loved."

As Luke and his three brothers came to understand the legacy their father had bequeathed to them, they enthusiastically embraced it. Nate played basketball at Princeton, while Adam wore the uniform of Cal Poly Pomona. Luke's youngest brother, Chris, now plays for San Diego State.

After playing at University High School in San Diego, Luke decided to go to the University of Arizona.

"The day I left the house," Luke said, "it was the first time I saw my dad cry since my last brother left for college."

At Arizona, Luke lived up to the high standards of the family name as he became one of only three players in Pac 10 history to have at least 1,000 career points, 500 rebounds, and 500 assists. Luke says his passion for the game and determination to succeed come from his father.

"When he was younger, he got into playing the piano," Luke said. "He'd wake up every morning at five and play from five to seven before he had to start doing other things. I'm the same way when it comes to basketball.

"I don't think that's just because of who my dad was. He used to tell us all the time, 'Find the passion for something and do that. You don't need to play basketball because I did.' I played all sports growing up. But my favorite happened to be basketball."

And as Luke continued to excel at each level, it became obvious he was going to have the chance to follow his father into the NBA.

Sure enough, he was selected by the Lakers with the

third pick in the second round, the thirty-second player selected overall.

Luke said, "It was awesome," watching the draft with his family on television. "For a while, it seemed like they said everybody's name but mine. And then finally, they said my first name. By the time they got to my last name, all my brothers were on me. My dad was just sitting up in his chair smiling."

Luke was feeling pretty good considering the success he had had in college and the fact that the NBA's glamour

franchise had selected him. But Bill wasn't about to let his son's head swell.

Luke recalled, "He told me, 'The NBA is the toughest league in the world. You are going to have to go out and work harder than you have ever worked, bring it every single day. But if you do make it, it's a great life and you'll meet great people.'"

Despite the presence of four superstars and the fact Jackson didn't like to play rookies, Luke managed to get into seventy-two regular-season games. But he started only two games, and averaged 10.1 minutes, 2.4 points, 1.8 rebounds, and 1.6 assists.

His father, of course, was his biggest cheerleader.

"If he saw that I was not playing much, or playing a bad game," Luke said, "he'd call me, leave a message, remind me that basketball is a game and meant to be fun. 'So,' he'd say, 'have fun with it.'"

Publicly, Bill might say harsher things. Because unlike other fathers, who could sit in the stands and root for their son, Bill often sat in front of a microphone in his capacity as a network analyst and had to give his audience an honest appraisal of what he was seeing.

And when it came to Luke, the harsh truth was not always flattering. Not that Luke would know firsthand.

"I knew better than to watch tapes of Laker games he was announcing," Luke said. "We're close and all, but I know that, when he's doing a game, he has a job to do behind the microphone, just like I'm out on the court doing a job.

"But I've gotten phone calls from my friends about stuff he's said. You know, like, 'That was a terrible pass by Walton. What was he thinking?'"

Luke could smile at such comments because he has seen both sides of his father.

"If you just see him on TV, he's always ripping people. He's hard on people," Luke said. "But as a dad, as a person around the neighborhood, he's really nice, a genuine guy. When my brothers and I were growing up playing basketball, a lot of our friends were underprivileged kids coming from the inner city. My dad would always help them out in high school, help them with financial things, take them into our house. We'd travel for games and maybe they couldn't afford the trip, so my dad would help them."

Therefore, no matter what he may have heard about his father's televised comments about his game, Luke had no doubt what his father really felt about him, especially after Luke played well in Game 2 of the NBA Finals against the Detroit Pistons.

"Everybody kept telling me how proud my dad looked," Luke said, referring to a shot of Bill in the stands on the national telecast. "I finally went back and watched the game, and, seeing how proud I had made him, that was a very special moment.

"He was just watching from the crowd. Now, if he had been working the game, I would have turned the volume down."

"No matter how this game comes out, you win. . . . You've gotten to where you want to be. Now just go out there and have fun."

FIVE

Bob and Brian Griese

FROM TRAGEDY TO TRIUMPH

When Bob Griese was ten years old his father died suddenly from a heart attack in his sleep. This left a hollow void—a dull ache in the young boy's heart. That's when Bob learned to keep his feelings private and keep his emotions in check. As quarterback for the Miami Dolphins, he was known as a cool, calm, stoic leader. A generation later Griese was a retired superstar turned successful broadcast announcer. But he was also a husband and a father, and when his wife Judi died of breast cancer, Bob Griese knew exactly how much his twelve-year-old son Brian hurt inside.

With Brian's oldest brother Scott already in college and Jeff heading off just months after his mother died, Brian was alone with his father in a household that had once bustled with the noise of two parents and three boys. Bob Griese recalled what his mother had done for him and strived to keep Brian's life as normal as possible—the daily routines, the schoolwork, the athletics. But he was

also willing to show his son the inner grieving that few others saw.

"We had a great relationship before my mother died," Brian recalls, but it was built largely on sports and competition. Afterward, his father showed him he could open up. "Our relationship shifted to a different dimension, toward being there for each other emotionally and being there to listen to the concerns we both had."

But the father-son relationship changed in another way as well, as Brian realized that emotional responsibility ran two ways in a family. "It made me grow up a lot faster and assume a lot more responsibility—to be mature enough to realize he needed me at that point in time," Brian says.

While Brian longed for a normal life, to just be a typical high school kid again—it didn't happen. For when he walked through the living room with his friends he'd see his dad alone, sitting silently, watching TV—and he just couldn't leave. "As much as I wanted to go out the door and jump in the car with my friends I couldn't do it because I didn't want to leave him by himself," he recalls. "He had lost his best friend . . . and I had to be that person now."

In 1990, two years after Judi died, Bob met Shay Whitney on a flight from Miami to Dallas and the two became friends. With Brian prodding his father to "get a life" and knowing that Judi had said he should not be alone but should remarry someday, Bob eventually asked Shay out—they were married in 1994.

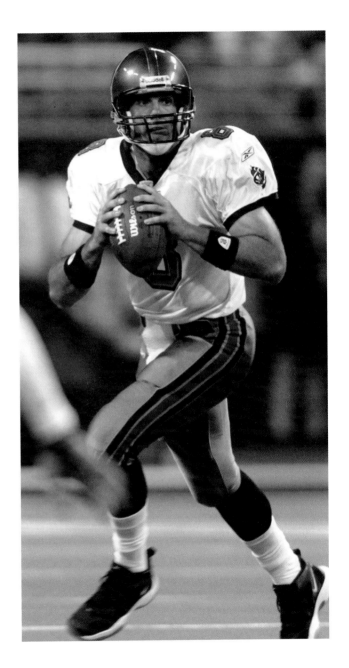

Meanwhile, the bond between father and son became so strong that when Brian achieved national fame on his own, his fondest memory was of sharing it publicly with his father.

Bob, of course, was already famous, beginning with his days as a two-time All-American at Purdue. He was heralded as "a thinking man's quarterback" with the Miami Dolphins. Although he never posted the gaudiest numbers, he was a savvy play caller and poised leader. (He also didn't need to throw deep all the time with Larry Csonka, Jim Kiick, and Mercury Morris to run the ball.) Most importantly, he helped lead Miami to three straight Super Bowls, including two championships—one of which capped their undefeated 1972 season. After he retired, the eight-time pro bowler was ushered into the Hall of Fame.

Bob never pressured his sons into sports. After Brian realized that he'd never make it in baseball, he developed into a stand-out football player at his father's old position, quarterback. In 1997, Brian led the University of Michigan to its own undefeated season. The season finale would be the Rose Bowl against the powerhouse Washington State team led by Ryan Leaf. And Bob Griese would be handling the broadcasting duties for ABC.

Before the game, Bob told Brian that he was in a situation where he could not lose. "No matter how this game comes out, you win. . . . You've gotten to where you want to be. Now just go out there and have fun." Bob said.

Brian appreciated the sentiment but remained a typically confident Griese, responding, "I'm gonna have fun, Pops—but I'm also going to win the Rose Bowl."

ABC had initially banned Bob from calling his son's games, concerned over conflict of interest, but eventually they'd relented since Bob had always been careful to be as objective as possible in his announcing.

But this time, the sixth time Bob would announce his son's game, would be different. Bob, of course, had won at the Rose Bowl himself, leading Purdue to a 14–13 win over USC in 1967. Now he watched as Brian threw an interception in the opening series of the game; the Wolverines were soon trailing 7–0. But Brian threw a beautiful fifty-three-yard touchdown pass in the second quarter and topped that with a fifty-eight-yarder in the third, one which prompted sideline reporter Lynn Swann to break the barrier and say, on the air, "Bob, my hat's off to your son." In the fourth quarter, Brian led a seventy-seven-yard drive that finished with a textbook twenty-four-yard touchdown pass and a seven-minute drive to protect the lead that included an eleven-yard run by Brian on third-and-eleven at his own eighteen-yard line.

As Washington made a last-ditch attempt to come back with twenty-nine seconds left, Brian stood on the sidelines and thought about his mother and felt her presence. When the clock finally ran down—leaving Michigan with a 21–16 win and a storybook undefeated season—Bob Griese finally lost his composure. He began

to cry on the air, no longer a Hall of Famer, or a professional announcer, just one thrilled and touched father.

"If you want to know who the Rose Bowl MVP is, I'm standing alongside his proud daddy," announcing partner Keith Jackson proclaimed as the ABC cameras captured Bob and Shay in a tearful embrace. Far from embarrassed, Brian was just as thrilled and touched by his father as Bob was by him. "Normally he's very reserved and analytical . . . but I was so proud of him at that moment and that's my best memory of him because he finally let his guard down," Brian remembers. "He showed all the viewers that he's not always the stoic figure and the 'thinking man's quarterback' but most importantly he is an emotional father and that's what that moment showed me."

And both Grieses soon proved that the openness, the willingness to expose raw emotion, was not fleeting, not something that just emerged in the heat of the competition they both loved so much. After the game, the Grieses were approached about writing a book about their undefeated seasons. These naturally private men were resistant at first but then, Brian said, "I thought about it for a while, and I went back to my dad and I said, 'If we have an opportunity to tell our story and what we went through both on the field and off the field with our relationships and one person reads the book and can gain some solace or maybe find a way to get through a grieving situation in their life, then it would be worth the time and effort to write the book.'"

The result—*Undefeated: How Father and Son Triumphed Over Unbelievable Odds Both On and Off the Field*—prompted so many letters and e-mails from readers that both Grieses were ultimately proud to have written it. "It went from a sports book to more of an emotional and a spiritual book," Brian said.

In the long run, understanding his emotions would also become crucial to Brian's professional success. Brian posted impressive numbers over four seasons with the Denver Broncos, but he was always compared to the legend who preceded him—not his father Bob, but the charismatic John Elway, who led the team to Super Bowl victories. Brian's passing rating and overall numbers were often better than Bob's or even Elway's.

Then he spent one unhappy season in Miami in 2003, where his father's shadow and the team's collapse into disarray left him without a starting job. Finally, in 2004, Brian emerged as his own man in Tampa Bay. He started off as the third-string quarterback, stuck behind veteran Brad Johnson and Chris Simms, the son of another legend (Phil Simms of New York Giants fame). It seemed he would have little chance to rewrite his place in football history, but when the team sputtered, Tampa coach Jon Gruden handed the starting job over to Griese. Brian promptly led them to three victories in his first four games. He not only led the offense, but he did it by unveiling a new, more emotional version of himself. After years of being known as the cool and calm quarterback in the mold of his father, Brian Griese has established himself as a fiery, finger-pointing leader.

And what of the relationship between father and son Griese? "I went through a lot of tough times," Brian said. "I was very angry at God, at society for not being able to cure cancer . . . angry at myself for not being a better son. I've grown so much since that time. And I think that my dad has grown as well in recognizing what things are important in life. So, from that standpoint our relationship has grown stronger, and probably more importantly, it's grown deeper."

"What he always told me was,
'Never be satisfied.' Whether I
pitched a perfect game or I gave up
two hits, there was always
something I could improve on."

SIX

Doug and Jennie Finch

RAISING A MONSTER
ON THE MOUND, A LADY IN LIFE

Who wouldn't want to be Jennie Finch? Who wouldn't want to have cover-girl looks that draw comparisons to Anna Kournikova and athletic talent sufficient to win an Olympic gold medal? Who wouldn't want to be a softball pitcher good enough to not only leave her peers awkward and helpless at the plate, but big-name major leaguers as well?

Jennie Finch, that's who. At one point, she would have traded it all in for a more routine existence. That was before she was a national and then international star, back when she was just the local whiz kid in La Mirada, California.

"I can remember," she said, "praying to God growing up, 'Why can't I just be normal? Why did you make me into this athlete? Why can't I go to birthday parties? Why can't I go to sleepovers?' I couldn't do those things because I had to be ready to leave for the softball field at five in the morning. And I was traveling all over the country."

Her father, Doug, kept a young Jennie on a course that would allow her to fulfill her destiny, before her own competitive juices kicked in.

Finch first threw a ball in competition at age five when her parents, Doug and Bev, signed her up for T-ball. However, she first realized that she was different

when her father moved her from her neighborhood team in La Mirada to a league in nearby Cypress where he felt the coaching was superior.

Finch was eight at the time, not ready to be separated from familiar faces or deal with the resentment of those she left behind.

"It kind of broke my heart," she said, "because I was leaving my friends and the people in my city. People were angry that I left because it was like I was too good for La Mirada.

"But my dad told me the Cypress league, 'wanted me to play and we want you to be the best that you can be.' I said, 'Nobody else among my friends is doing this.' And he said, 'You're not like everybody else. You're special.'

"I didn't think I was special. I thought I had the worst life on earth. All I did was eat, breathe, and sleep softball and I thought that was all my dad cared about. He didn't care about me. He just cared about softball. But sure enough, everything worked out. He was right. He saw the potential I had, something I didn't see at the time."

As the years passed, that potential became more and more obvious.

At La Mirada High School, Finch was All-CIF (California Interscholastic Federation), named three times first-team, all-league, was a two-time league Most Valuable Player, and her school's Female Athlete of the Year in 1998. She finished her high school career with a 50–12 record, six perfect games, thirteen no-hitters, an 0.15 ERA, and 784 strikeouts.

And through it all, her father was her driving force. He built a batting cage in their backyard and designed a device to exercise her pitching arm, sold today as the Finch Windmill.

"What he always told me was, 'Never be satisfied.' Whether I pitched a perfect game or I gave up two hits, there was always something I could improve on. Always, after the game, he would say, 'Good job.' But then, there was this, this, this, and this, he'd tell me that I needed to work on during the week for next week.

"He would push me and push me and push me, but he never pushed too far. People say, 'How do you know when it's too far?' I don't know, but I know some of my friends hated the sport because of their parents pushing them too far."

When Jennie was eleven, she thought her father was close to pushing too far. She had told him that an injury to a finger on her pitching hand was too sore to allow her to pitch. With her team in a national tournament, Finch found that the tight grip she would continue to use in her motion had already worn the skin down to the bone.

It didn't matter. Her father pushed her out on the mound.

"My finger was just thrashed open," she said. "I tuck that finger on a lot of my pitches and it was bleeding, the worst throbbing pain ever. I said, 'Dad, I can't do it.' He said, 'You can do it. You know this is what you've worked for. After the game, you won't remember how bad it hurts.'

"As I was warming up, the pain was excruciating and I was crying. Again, I told my dad, I couldn't do it and he said I could. He told my coach, 'She's ready and she's going to pitch.'

"Sure enough, once I stepped on the field and threw the first pitch, I couldn't feel my finger any longer."

Jennie had a similar experience at the University of Arizona. Even with an injury to a bone in the forearm of her pitching hand, she still went out to pitch as she had with that bleeding finger.

"You just have to get past the warm-ups," she said, "because once you step on the field, your adrenaline takes over and you look at your teammates and you

know how hard they worked and how hard you've worked and you come together for your goal."

Finch reached every goal imaginable in college. Arizona reached the NCAA Women's College World Series all four years she was on the team, winning the championship in 2001. She is a two-time winner of the Honda Award (2001–02), given to the nation's top softball player. When it comes to winning, she was unequaled. Finch won an NCAA record sixty consecu-

tive games over a three-year span at Arizona. The streak began after Jennie gave up a game-winning home run.

"I told myself that I didn't ever want to feel that way again," she said.

While most collegiate softball players wind up their career with graduation, Finch has continued to find bigger and bigger targets at which to fire her windmill arm. Representing her country, she was on gold-medal winning teams at the 2003 Pan Am Games in the

Dominican Republic and the 2004 Olympics in Athens.

Finch looked down from the platform while receiving Olympic gold and saw her parents.

"Their whole lives were softball," she said. "Everything we did, our whole house was softball. And finally, it all kind of made sense."

Finch has also worked as commentator and analyst for ESPN, which included pitching to major league hitters like Larry Walker, Paul Lo Duca, and Scott Spiezio. Anyone who may have scoffed at the idea of facing a young woman soon learned that a softball, coming from only forty-three feet—the distance from mound to plate in softball—at a speed of seventy-one miles per hour can be even more difficult than facing a Randy Johnson or a

Roger Clemens. Major leaguers soon learned that getting a foul tip off Finch was something to brag about.

While Jennie can thank her father for pushing her to all her achievements on the diamond, she feels he was also responsible for her becoming one of sport's glamour figures and being voted ESPN's Hottest Female Athlete.

"My dad loves makeup on me," Finch said. "He loves seeing me dressed up. He even did my hair in pigtails when I was little. He was the one who encouraged me to be feminine. He likes it that I wear makeup on the mound, but still go out there and get the job done. That's where he gets his pride, in the fact that I'm a girl, but I can play ball and get down and dirty on the field."

And today, despite all Finch has accomplished, her father is still there, keeping her from getting complacent.

"He's still working with me," Finch said, "catching me and coaching me. I still don't have the perfect mechanics, so it definitely continues to be a process. I'm so blessed to still have him there for me. I'm throwing seventy miles an hour and he's still back there catching me.

"He was the one who made me better, made me one of the best in the country and able to make the Olympic team. I look back at all the hours he spent and all the sacrifices in his life he made for me and I'm so grateful."

SEVEN

Ned and Dale Jarrett

FATHER AND SON, FRIENDS TO THE FINISH

This is a story about a boy named Dale who grew up to be a famous race car driver, just like his daddy. No, not that Dale. Racing is a sport rich in father-son tandems, but while the Earnhardts have attracted the most attention in recent years, Ned and Dale Jarrett rank among the sport's famous and closest families. Their crowning accomplishment—Dale winning the Daytona 500 with Ned cheering him on in the broadcast booth—is one of the most memorable in the hard-bitten, macho world of NASCAR racing.

When Dale Jarrett was a boy he'd sit in his parents' car and pretend to be driving—and winning—the Daytona 500. It's a fantasy many kids indulge in, especially if their daddy drives race cars. Dale often palled around with Kyle Petty, Davey Allison, and Ricky and Larry Pearson. But what was unusual about Dale's choice was that his father was a Hall of Fame driver who captured fifty titles and two Winston Cup championships . . . yet he never won at Daytona.

Ned, however, considered himself lucky to be racing at all. His father expected him to go into the family lumber business—they'd worked in the sawmills around Hickory, North Carolina, for generations. In those days racing was connected more to liquor bootlegging than national television deals. "My dad worked very hard to build a lot of respect and a good image," Ned once recalled, explaining why he started by sneaking out to help a friend race before venturing into the car himself. The first time on the track was an accident. "My partner got sick. We went out into the infield and changed shirts. I put on his helmet. We figured nobody would know the difference."

Racing as 'John Lentz,' Ned finished second and no one was the wiser. But when he soon started winning races, his dad quickly found out in small-town Hickory. "He told me if I was so determined to drive one of those things, I might as well use my own name and get credit for any accomplishments," Ned has explained. "He became one of my biggest fans."

"Gentleman Ned" eventually drove his way onto the NASCAR circuit, winning fifty of 352 races while lending a touch of class to the fledgling sport. "He showed we weren't all rednecks," Richard Petty once said, of Jarrett's competitive but clean approach.

Ned would often bring his entire family along to races, but even when his mom, Martha, and other children would stay home, Dale always wanted to tag along until his dad retired at age thirty-four, just before Dale was ten.

Ned Jarrett had accomplished a great deal but the one thing Ned never did was win at Daytona, although he finished in the top five six times and in 1963 was winning when he ran out of gas with only three laps to go.

Ned went into broadcasting, but still Dale was more removed from the sport than other racing progeny whose fathers kept racing. In fact, it seemed as if Dale would move away from racing entirely. At Newton-Conover High School he was the star quarterback, shortstop, and forward in the three big team sports. He was also a superb golfer and for a while Dale seemed to be heading toward golf. Ned thought this was fine since he saw his eldest son,

Glenn, as the Jarrett who'd carry on the racing tradition.

Ned urged Dale to take golf seriously and aim for the PGA Tour. "Dale had a lot of God-given talent as an athlete," Ned once said. "The reason I wanted him to pursue golf was that I knew the pitfalls of racing. I knew the hardships and sacrifices he would have to make."

Fortunately for Ned, teenage sons often ignore their fathers and while Glenn was proving to be more of a crasher than a driver on the race course, Dale would eventually leave his drivers on the golf course and take the wheel. (Glenn went on to succeed as a racing broadcaster.)

Dale turned down a golf scholarship to the University of South Carolina, in part, Ned has said, "because he wasn't much interested in studying" and in part, his son said, because golf seemed more fraught with anxiety than the world of racing. "A pro golfer is totally by himself; I can't imagine the pressure of making a three-foot putt for a win," Dale has said. "My sport's dangerous, but I have a steel frame protecting me and an entire team to help me get to the checkered flag."

Still, Dale floundered after high school. He got married, had a son, Jason, and divorced quickly. He went to work for his dad, who then ran the Hickory Motor Speedway, but he did odd jobs: ticket taker, popcorn seller, pace car driver, lawn mower.

Finally, when Dale was twenty he began working on a race car with some friends and persuaded Ned to front him the money to buy an engine. Ned was able to help out and his name still opened some doors. However, he was too far removed from his racing days to provide the connections and financial support that the children of other racers received. "I'm glad it worked out in that way because he learned it all on his own," Ned has said. "He had to work hard for everything he's got."

Once Dale got behind the wheel it didn't matter how hard he would have to work—after starting twenty-fifth and finishing ninth in his first race Dale felt the calling. That was in 1977, but it would take seven years of determination and hard work before he drove his first Winston Cup race in 1984. He mostly raced in the Busch series from 1982 on but his first Busch win wasn't until 1986 (he'd win ten more races on that circuit). Dale started racing Winston Cup full time in 1987, but his only win before his Daytona breakthrough in 1993 came in 1991. He was doing what he loved and never felt pressure to compete with his father's track record. "I never came into this thing thinking to be successful that I had to win fifty races and two championships like my dad."

Ned, while always a close and steadying influence, was never one to interfere or push Dale too hard to do things his way. "The one thing he has learned from me is patience," Ned has said. "That is a key factor in this business. That was sort of my philosophy when I drove race cars."

Patience gave him enough experience that allowed his natural skills to eventually shine. And he picked one memorable race to break through: the 1993 Daytona 500.

Ned Jarrett had done radio calls for the Daytona 500

after retiring in 1966, and he had announced every race since CBS began national telecasts in 1979. But this one would be different. Ironically, Dale's greatest moment in his lime-green No. 18 came at the expense of that other Dale—the legendary Earnhardt Sr., who at the time was like Ned with impeccable credentials but no wins at Daytona.

Earnhardt was in the lead with just twenty-six laps to go and Ned was in the booth with Neil Bonnett and Ken Squires, trying to maintain his objectivity. Toward the end of the race, the CBS producer told the mild-mannered Ned to take over and just let himself go. So in the last lap, with the two Dales side by side Ned cheered, "It's Dale and Dale as they come off Turn 4!" Jarrett said on air. "And you know who I'm pulling for.

"Come on, Dale! Go, baby, go! I know he's gone to the floorboard. He can't do any more. Come on, take her to the inside. Don't let him get on the inside of you comin' around the turn. Bring her to the inside, Dale; don't let him get down there. He's gonna make it. Dale Jarrett's gonna win the Daytona 500! All right! Look at Martha. Oh, can you believe it!"

Later on Ned would say, "I thought he could hear what I was saying."

The cameras gave viewers the full emotional story cutting from Dale to Ned—who would later say that was "the greatest feeling I've ever had"—grinning gleefully in the booth to Martha, who was barely able to contain her joy.

Afterward, Ned "interviewed" Dale, whose $238,200 payday nearly matched his father's eleven-year total. "Super job, Dale! I'm really proud of you! You did just exactly what you had to—just like I told you, right?"

Dale, who has always said his dad was his "hero," readily agreed. "Exactly like you've told me all along. Thanks a lot for everything. . . . I thought we'd get this one for the whole family."

Three years later Dale Jarrett would again win the Daytona 500 with his father announcing. Eventually he'd win it a third time and finally capture a Winston Cup title, making the Jarretts only the second father-son duo (after the Pettys) to have attained that milestone. And when Dale would hit the occasional slump, he always knew who to turn to: Ned. "He's been my biggest supporter, and it's great to have a dad and a friend who knows enough about the sport that he can help you," he once said.

Years later, Ned once commented that in retrospect the 1993 race had only grown in its place in family and NASCAR lore. "We didn't realize how much a part of history that would become at the time.

"It's something we get a lot of comments about from people, still to this day," Dale has said, adding that the day now carries extra meaning because he is now the father of a race car driver—Jason— and understands the pride his father must have felt in his accomplishment.

But perhaps the lasting image of that day back in 1993 should come from the aftermath, when the excitement died down and Ned felt bad about his cheerleading from the booth. He sought out Dale Earnhardt to apologize. "He said, 'I'm a daddy, too,'" Jarrett said then. "He just removed all of those bad thoughts that I'd had about the race. It choked me up."

But while he set no records in the 2003
season, in its own searing and indelible
way, that season is the one for which he
deserves to be remembered—the year
he demonstrated that he could be both
a son and a star all at once.

EIGHT

Barry and Bobby Bonds

A GIANT FOLLOWING IN A GIANT'S FOOTSTEPS

Bobby Bonds helped create the greatest player of our generation in more ways than one. As a talented ballplayer in his own right, Bonds certainly passed on his fair share of genes and baseball knowledge to his son Barry, in addition to a close relationship with none other than Willie Mays, Barry's godfather.

But Bobby Bonds also endured perhaps more than his fair share of criticism from both fans and the media—he, like many others before and since, failed to live up to the hype of being the "next" Willie Mays—and that in turn hardened his son, to the point where Barry became notorious as one of the least popular men in baseball.

Then, in 2003, as Bobby lay dying, he bequeathed one final gift to his son, inadvertently softening Barry's public image. As Barry went from his father's bedside to the ballpark, winning games in near-miraculous fashion, all the while brimming with emotion, he finally allowed fans to see the humanity beneath the hard shell.

The elder Bonds burst on the scene with Mays' San Francisco Giants in June 1968, becoming the first modern player to hit a grand slam in his first major league game. The following year, in Bonds's first full season, the Giants moved him into the leadoff spot and he flaunted a combo of speed and power that, outside of Mays and Mickey Mantle, had hardly ever been seen before. He hit thirty-two homers, stole forty-five bases, drove in ninety runs, and scored 120 more. But he also showed a

lack of discipline that would haunt him in years to come, striking out 187 times that season to set a new record for futility. The record did not last long—in 1970, Bonds struck out 189 times.

"They said I was supposed to be the next Willie Mays," Bonds once snapped. "When they told me that, it was an honor. You're talking about a guy who I considered the greatest player to ever wear shoes. I probably had more success than anyone they ever put that label on. . . . But all the writers kept talking about was potential. You haven't reached your potential, they say. Well, unless you win a Pulitzer Prize, you're not living up to your potential either, are you?"

Bonds lived in the shadow of the beloved and well-rounded Mays. Although he produced All-Star seasons in 1971 and 1973 (with thirty-nine homers and forty-three steals in the latter year), the perception was that it was never enough—and indeed his play, effort, and attitude certainly suffered because of his drinking problem. He would not tackle his alcoholism until after his playing days were over. Bonds was traded to the New York Yankees, where he roamed center field, the spot once held by Mantle and Joe DiMaggio. He made the All-Star team but was traded anyway to the California Angels. Between 1976 and 1981, he would subsequently be shipped to the Chicago White Sox, Texas Rangers, Cleveland Indians, St. Louis Cardinals, and Chicago Cubs. Still, in the end, he hit thirty homers for five different teams and finished with an impressive tally of 332.

When Barry was a young star, Bobby and Barry were both angry at the possibility that the burdens heaped on the father would also be heaped on the son. "Now, I see it again," Bobby said. "I tell you what you're doing, you're destroying a young ballplayer. You don't realize what you're doing, but you're putting him in a position to fail. . . . Tell me how fair that is."

Except, of course, Barry Bonds did not fail. With an abstemiousness and devotion to his craft that more resembled Mays, he surpassed all imaginable expectations, becoming perhaps the greatest slugger baseball has ever known as well as a defensive standard setter. But along the way, he seemed to alienate just about everyone in his path. Some of that came from being Bobby's son—and not just because of anger at the way the media had treated his father. Barry was born when Bobby was only a month out of high school. And while Barry grew up with plenty of money and a childhood that included following Mays around the locker room, he was not close with his father, who not only drank but who could also be quite hard on his son. (Bobby once supposedly said to Barry, "You're fast, but you're only the third-fastest person in the family. I'm faster than you, and your aunt can beat you, too." Bonds's aunt Rosie was a former Olympian who held an American record in women's hurdles.)

"I didn't like my dad that much," Bonds has said.

It only grew worse when Bobby began his midcareer odyssey, leaving his wife and children, including Barry, then ten, in the Bay Area. It wasn't until after Bobby retired from baseball that their relationship developed. "We didn't become close until I was in college. I resented him when I was a kid. Not that he was abusive. There's a fine line between abuse and discipline."

"He never came to my games until I was in college," Barry once said. They first grew close when Barry starred at Arizona State University. Bobby was coaching in Cleveland then and would spend spring training in Arizona, visiting with and watching his son. Eventually Bobby was the only person he would trust to tinker with his swing.

In the majors, the left-handed slugger did not get off to as fast a start as his dad and after his first four years he was known more for his moodiness and contract demands than for his on-field production. That changed in the 1990s. From 1990 to 1994, Bonds won three Most Valuable Player Awards in four years, with that same combination of speed and power possessed by his father and godfather. In the midst of that MVP run, he returned home to San Francisco as a free agent, signing what was then an astronomical $43 million contract for seven years. Barry was truly coming home, since the Giants hired proud Bobby as hitting coach, where he served the next four years, before becoming a scout and special assistant to the general manager. No matter what his position, he was firmly established as Barry's confidant and hitting guru.

Barry was also collecting Gold Gloves in left field on an almost annual basis. With his father in the dugout, he

also became the first National League player to hit forty home runs and steal forty bases in a single season (his father had once missed by one homer) while drawing 151 walks, an indicator that he had the patience and plate discipline that his father never possessed.

At the end of the 1990s, Bonds was the *Sporting News'* player of the decade. That was no surprise. But by then, everyone thought his Hall of Fame career was on the downward slide. Little did they know he was about to get better. In 2001, at age thirty-seven, he shattered all single season records with seventy-three home runs. The next year, although he was routinely being pitched around, he hit .370 to win his first batting title, then smashed eight home runs and drew twenty-seven walks in a postseason run that nearly led the Giants to the World Series title.

In those two years fans began to see glimpses of the

man behind the image of the arrogant $90 million prima donna. In 2001, he brought his daughter, Aisha, to press conferences and kept his focus despite death threats and the deaths of a cousin, uncle, and bodyguard. During the 2002 series, he kept his son, Nikolai, by his side in the locker room. (Bonds's private image is often at odds with his public one. In the past, he has earned Philanthropist of the Year honors from the National Conference on Black Philanthropy and has been honored for work with the Adopt-A-Special-Kid program and the Cardiac Arrhythmias Research and Education Foundation.)

In 2003, Bonds was rapidly closing in on Mays for third on the all-time home run list, but now the emotional burden was unlike anything he had experienced—he was helplessly watching his father slowly wither away. Bobby Bonds had suffered through tumor surgery on his brain, kidney, and heart as he battled an aggressive lung cancer. Now, Barry would routinely rush from the ballpark after home games to be with his father. That he continued to produce at his own elevated pace was nothing short of remarkable.

As the summer wore on and Bobby's health grew worse, Barry's focus seemed, astonishingly, to improve. In mid-August, he took time off to be with his father. While he was gone, the Giants—in the thick of a pennant race—mustered only four runs in losing four straight games. On August 19, Bonds came back and promptly lifted the team with a game-winning 457-foot home run in the tenth inning.

Before the game, Bonds, a bit choked up, spoke publicly about his father, saying graciously and humbly, "It was important for me to be there with my dad at this time. It's also important for me to be here [at the ballpark] as well. I'll do the best I can to do both. I just hope everyone understands.

"My dad wants everybody to know that he thanks them for all their support. . . . He wishes he could be here on a regular basis. But unfortunately, he can't do that right now."

Perhaps even more revealing was the comment he made after his game-winning home run, which he celebrated by pointing skyward even before the ball had left the park. "I owe the Braves an apology. . . . The early celebration like that, I hope they don't take offense to it. I just had a lot of emotions going through me for my dad."

Suddenly, it seemed baseball fans and sportswriters everywhere were on Bonds's side. The next night, Bobby Bonds attended the game and was treated to an extended ovation from the fans when a message flashed: "A Giant Welcome to Bobby Bonds, Three-Time All-Star."

Barry, showing he was human but not superhuman, was distracted by his father's presence, constantly looking up toward his private booth. Barry went hitless, his finest contribution was the sign on the scoreboard to the twenty-four people he had invited to the game: "Barry Bonds and his family want to thank the Stanford Medical Center doctors and nurses [at] tonight's game."

And the next night? Barry again won the game with a tenth-inning home run. But while Barry could control the on-field script with astonishing skill, unfortunately, this is not a fairy tale with a happy ending—on August 23, Bobby died.

The Giants donned black patches with BB to honor Bobby, but Barry created his own special tribute to his father, one which further cemented his heroic performance as one for the ages. Bonds missed another six games after his father died then returned against Randy Johnson—baseball's most dominating left-handed pitcher—and homered. That would spark a 2–1 victory, but Bonds was growing light-headed and suffering heart palpitations while rounding the bases; he left the game in the eighth inning with his heart pounding at twice the normal rate. He was hospitalized the next day for exhaustion. But one day later, Bonds was back and in the ninth inning of a scoreless game he knocked in two runs to lead his team to another crucial victory.

Bonds would largely go back to being his own private self, yet he would make emotionally open com-ments like admitting he spent much of the 2003 season "just trying not to have a nervous breakdown." At the season's end, Bonds won an unprecedented sixth MVP award, having hit forty-five homers and walking 148 times in only 130 games.

Although allegations of steroids use have dogged Bonds, his accomplishments are beyond Ruthian—they are, for want of a better word, Bondsian. In 2004, his seventh MVP season, Bonds hit another forty-five homers, racked up a record-smashing 232 walks and only forty-one strikeouts, and earned his second batting title at .362. In 2005, he expects to pass Babe Ruth on the all-time home run list; in 2006, he may well top Hank Aaron to become the king. But while he set no records in the 2003 season, in its own searing and indelible way, that season is the one for which he deserves to be remembered—the year he demonstrated that he could be both a son and a star all at once.

CREDITS

Authored and produced by Joe Garner

Editorial/text assistance provided by Stuart Miller, Todd Schindler, and Bill Stroum

Narration by Joe Garner

Original music score composed and orchestrated by Richard Kosinski

Production coordinator, photo editor, and assistant to Joe Garner: Abigail Ray

DVD supervising editor: Chris Monte, Magic Hair Inc.

Audio production engineering by Tree Falls, Los Angeles, California

Main title, animation, and menu design by Castle Digital Design

Creative director: James Castle

Senior animator: Robert Dixon

DVD authoring provided by Los Angeles Duplication and Broadcast, Burbank, California

Footage provided by:

ABC Sports

HBO Sports

Major League Baseball Productions

NASCAR Images

NBA Entertainment

NFL Network © 2005

We would like to express our heartfelt gratitude to all of the announcers who have graciously permitted the inclusion of their thrilling calls.